BORDER DISPUTES

To Kelvin
with all best wishes
Charles Hadfield
December 1996

First published in 1995 by *Salzburg University*
in its series:
SALZBURG STUDIES IN ENGLISH LITERATURE
POETIC DRAMA & POETIC THEORY

116

EDITOR: JAMES HOGG

ISBN   3-7052-0430-0

INSTITUT FÜR ANGLISTIK UND AMERIKANISTIK
UNIVERSITÄT SALZBURG
A-5020 SALZBURG
AUSTRIA

Cover Drawing © Ian Robinson 1995.

DRAKE

INTERNATIONAL SERVICES

MARKET HOUSE, MARKET PLACE, DEDDINGTON, OXFORD OX15 0SF

TELEPHONE/FAX: 01869 338240

BORDER DISPUTES

poems by

CHARLES HADFIELD

with forewords
by
Yann Lovelock
and
Andrea Moorhead

UNIVERSITY OF SALZBURG
1995

For Jill

ACKNOWLEDGEMENTS

I wish to thank the editors of the following magazines for publishing poems in this collection over the last few years:

Acumen, The Beau (Dublin), *Blue Cage, Coelacanth Press* (Dublin), *Iron, Krino* (Galway), *Limestone - Strange Fruit, Literaturen Vestnik* (Sofia), *Mosaic, Negative Entropy, Ninth Decade, Oasis, Odyssey, Osiris* (U.S.A), *Pearl, Poésie Europe* (Frankfurt), *Poesis, Poetry Durham, Poetry Review, Resurgence, Reynard, The Rialto, Rind und Schlegel* (Frankfurt), *Shearsman, South West Review, Sow's Ear, Strange Mathematics, Stride* and *Westwords*.

CONTENTS

vi

Charles Hadfield: A First Encounter
by YANN LOVELOCK

I still remember vividly the impact of practically the first poems Charles Hadfield had published. They appeared in a 1981 issue of *Limestone*, placed after the reviews and thus divided from work by the usual run of contributors, as if to emphasize the strangeness of this new voice. The editor knew nothing about him. The poems had appeared out of the blue, he told me, and so impressed him that he decided to use all of them. There the matter might have rested, new poets come and go as frequently as the little magazines in which they appear, and I have a short-term memory for names. Later that summer I went to the wedding of a friend, an EFL teacher in Torquay and, introduced to a colleague, asked him if he was *the* Charles Hadfield. We have kept in touch ever since.

Of those six early poems, four, ("Snow Poem" "Abstract Light" "Just A Moment" "Summer Funeral") are included in this collection. They were not quite Charlie's debut. "Weather" and "Midwinter" had appeared in *Poetry Review* in the autumn of 1979, but nothing in between. It seemed marvellous that so assured a style had been achieved without the usual fumbling that most of us go through. There was too their mysterious quality, an engagement with both language and reality, always broken off before the disfiguring moment of didacticism. This left the poems open to new readings, they were always fresh. The way sentences simply broke off in the middle, veering away from the obvious, was a trick he might have learned from Lee Harwood, except that Harwood (at the time) was more concerned with language's creation of the fictitious. Hadfield, on the other hand, was very definitely concerned with the detail of the here and now and what might be made of it.

Few of us could have guessed at the time the influence of Philippe Jaccottet, on whom Charlie had written his MA thesis. The bilingual Penguin selection of his poems was not published until 1988. Even then, if one sticks to the rather plonking English versions there, their kinship is hardly obvious. It is the spirit of the French originals that breathes through Hadfield's poems. This is not to say that he goes in for mere imitation. It is true that there is a similar obsession with qualities of light, and with the limitations of what can be expressed. Both agree that the emotional stirrings prompted by certain circumstances, the meanings one intuits, can only be conveyed by depicting such scenes with a chaste economy of language –

> Everything must be written once
> then twice with the same words.

But what gives life to Hadfield's poetry is that he writes in terms of his own experience. The details are English, recognisably our own in their humility, as is the language used to express through them the unsayable.

Although Hadfield found his own voice early, his aesthetic was a limited one and did not travel particularly well. Of his Chinese poems, "Qu Yuan" is not at ease with the new surroundings, its exotic chinoiserie obscuring its deeper point of departure in a way the English poems never did, while "Meeting the Buddha" reads more like a tourist poem in the manner of Arthur Whaley. Obviously a new approach was needed in order to express the deep impressions left by his prolonged experience of China, Tibet and Madagascar.

The new quality that has entered his later work is a hardening of mood. The irony there is neither playful nor bitter, but one of acceptance. His former tenderness of spirit, which, in Lee Harwood's work too often degenerates into sentimentality whenever he tries to engage with real life, has been tempered by anger into a true compassion. Several titles might be cited in illustration, but for me the most telling indication of this new mood is in "Attention! Un train peut en cacher un autre". This poem, growing out of his Tibetan experience, could not present a greater contrast to his 'Chinese' manner.

There has been a stylistic shift, also, or rather a second voice is now heard. The formative encounter in this case has been with the writing of John Ashbery, one that has had fruitful results in the work of other English poets. In the case of John Ash it freed him from a mannered formalism and allowed him to romp at ease among English cultural references of the most diverse kind. David Grubb's somewhat stilted surrealism was given an extended range and new fluency. Hadfield's debts to Ashbery include the formal (the addition of prose poems to his repertoire, for instance) and the ability to cover a variety of experiences in poems held together by unity of mood. Formerly a single instance informed poems that were short, crafted and lyrical. Now he is prepared to take risks in lines that are longer and more rhetorical, in poems of greater complexity and breadth.

Incredibly, this is Hadfield's first collection. One cannot count *16 Poems*, the booklet he published himself in order to have something to sell during a reading he did for *Poésie Europe* at the 1986 Frankfurt bookfair. Indeed, it is practically his first solo performance, since the EFL texts and travel books were co-authored by his wife Jill. In the generous space allotted here are really the matter for two collections, whose qualities I have tried to indicate. Naturally there are continuities, and it is fascinating to see how the one blends into the other. In the fifteen years I have been following Charlie's work, I have been surprised over and over again by the new directions it has taken. Not many – a few editors apart – have had this privilege. I find myself envying his new readers the freshness of their first encounter.

Permutations of Memory in Charles Hadfield's *Cartographies* by ANDREA MOORHEAD

I first became aware of Charles Hadfield's work when we published his long poem *Cartographies* in *Osiris 35* in 1992. I was intrigued by the mapping out of autobiographical details and the subtle permutations of memory. The opening lines "*We create our own cities/ in the sad spaces of the heart*" stand out as the legend for the psychological mapping of reality rather than as a lyrical cry or a statement of personal concerns or conditions. Hadfield uses a series of overlapping transparencies to create a dense personal reality that is free of explicit autobiographical statement. The images are drawn from distant cities whose internal landscapes perturb the poet's memory. The function of memory is integrated into the cityscapes which are themselves devoid of confessional or intimate content. The *sad spaces* evoked become entire worlds that flow one into the other. *Trust memory for all you need/ and so we create our own sad cities*. The poem recreates its own internal landscapes from section to section, resolving the ambiguously entertained fragments in the final section with subtle irony.

Hadfield uses the natural landscape as anaphora. The images from his extensive travels are imbedded in the poetical narrative. An extended reverie, a phantasmagorical background (a public reception, a ballroom) become the grounds from which merge both defined characters and specific elements of the landscape. The sudden interjection of specific spatial coordinates (*we changed trains at the border*) and the reference to specific contemporary historical moments (*war is brewing*) give the poem its forward vector. The poetic details are deleted, suspended, thus allowing the reader to muse on the reality alluded to by the text and still entertain the primary aesthetic concerns of the formal text.

True orange/ is a quality of light concludes a graceful and evocative section that suddenly emerges from the poem's rather journalistic style. The splintered fragments of landscape are pulled together, the emotional waves with metaphoric impact are tamed, tucked into the poem's main structure, made to present the refined surface of the civilized world.

The final section of the poem is a recapitulation of all the preceding elements. Its dovetailed symmetry is a beautifully crafted example of modern classicism. All the fragments of vision, observation, thought, conjecture, and analysis are brought together and realigned. The great physical distances in the poem are used as elements in a fugue. The language of the poem is almost *new lyric* at times. It shifts, drops, changes focus and intensity. Fragments of phrases, unaligned words, parenthetical remarks are all woven together to provide texture, setting and intensity. The clarity of voice comes from the delicately detailed landscapes that act as a dynamic foreground for the more complex social concerns of the main text. *Cartographies* maps out a dense multi-cultural reality that is altered as the light on the landscape subtly shifts and changes.

I do not suggest that these remarks be taken as a formal analysis of Hadfield's *Cartographies*. I would like to signal an editor's enthusiasm for a poet who risks a great deal in his writing. The task of taming and refining so many seemingly contradictory vectors is daunting. Hadfield's language is clean, clear, and carefully worked. He moves through the various voice lines, at times losing the sharpness of a transition, at times unravelling the text a bit too far. There is a gentleness of tone and a clarity of judgement that appeal in these texts. Despite the dark side of contemporary reality, the reader feels assured that Charles Hadfield holds his fellow human beings in great respect. His charge as a poet is to integrate the seemingly antagonistic social and physical realities he experiences into a coherent vision. His message for his reader is one of community : *we create our own cities/ in the sad spaces of the heart.* These *sad spaces* are shared realities. Intimacy comes from the shared spaces, from the jarring fault lines between realities, from the oddly overlapping discordances of the heart. Poetic reality arises from the happy collaboration of the mime artist, the landscape painter, the amateur photographer, the reporter on special assignment, the educator and the dreamer.

(Andrea Moorhead is editor of *OSIRIS*.)

'ABSTRACT LIGHT'

- an introduction to BORDER DISPUTES

For me, creating a poem is one of the most satisfying activities possible. It stretches me, to work on a series of words until I can get them no further in draft form (most of my writing is abandoned at some point, rather than completed, and only a handful of the poems here are what I would regard as fully 'finished'). It is an inching towards the truth - towards *a* truth, for there are many possible truths, or facets of what may be true. It is a form of honesty of perception, of clarity, of 'truth to the moment'. So it combines good faith, common sense, and I hope a working towards rather than away from the light. We only live once (as far as can be certain) and this short existence is not to be wasted. Writing poems is a valuable use of this time for me, as it is an attempt to crystallize, or find the essence, of all the wonderfully diverse experiences possible.

I cannot draw or paint, but photography is important to me. I suspect that many of the pictures my words try to describe, are in fact 'photos' of abstract concepts which are inexpressible outside the world of the poem. Verbal images of the physical external world are, like photographs, representations of 'reality'. But once you begin to introduce abstract ideas, representation becomes difficult - perhaps I am trying to photograph what is impossible to photograph.

Music is also extremely important to me. In a sense music is the opposite of photography: while photography records precisely what is before the lens at any chosen time, music is almost entirely self-referential, yet I find it the most expressive of all the arts. Are my poems then an attempt to photograph abstract concepts, and to express in language the wordless truths of music?

I find it hard to list the poets or other writers who have influenced me, partly because whoever I listed, I would inevitably regret missing someone out. However, I have studied French and European literature, and am very conscious of my debt to certain French poets, especially Jaccottet. I am pleased that many of my poems and prose pieces have appeared over the years in the multi-lingual magazines, *Poésie Europe* and *Osiris*, for I hope that my writing, while in English, is international in its outlook. Wherever I've travelled I've always tried to learn new languages (without too much success, but with great interest) and I find the 'otherness' of new words and languages exciting and enriching:

> 'I start to translate, working one speech into another,
> and attempting new scripts (...) There no language
> but strange mathematics waiting for proofs.'
> *Learning to Read Again*

Looking back on these pieces, as I tried to select them, I often thought to myself 'yes, I remember vividly how I came to write that' - but having written one poem in a certain way does not mean you can ever repeat the performance - I have no set recipes or methods of writing. Some of these poems came to me complete, or nearly so, and required very little later work. Others have taken much longer to reach their present state (the longest here took 12 years). The truths worth telling are always changing, inspirations are many and various, always a surprise, always a mystery. Fresh words which grow into fresh poems always come as a shock to me.

And then there is always more to say, another way of putting it, a nearer approach to perfection (which is impossible to attain):

> 'It is to withold information
> (to not tell the truth)
> as it itches behind your eyes
> to achieve this balance
> between joy and sadness....'
> *Fountains*

Charles Hadfield, Devon, November 1994

CROWD CONTROL

Of all the puzzles, it's words
that are hardest to understand.

Looking up meanings,
the possibilities of nuance grow

and the dictionary is useless
unless by some chance,

meditating at sunset
on a tropical beach,

the thing itself is there
in front of you

lighting vast fires
beyond the calm sea.

How rarely is it possible
to say 'this' and not 'that'

(but a wave of the hand
from a passing stranger

or a look, even,
is far more worrying).

SWEEPING UP

There's always a first time:
"It came as a complete surprise"

(the difference between what was expected
and what they actually did)

yet, the morning after, looking
through the trees in the pale winter light

as the vans come and go,
the different uniforms collecting evidence,

all these strangers who know
so much more than the neighbours

"Always said hello, quite friendly."
"Nine years was it? No, ten."

it all fits into place.
Retrospective logic making sense,

the loose snapshots
stuck in the album.

EXILES

Help! you scream
through the perfection of eyes
meeting
at once we shy off
but if our fingers
once touched
no one would know
how

and as trains
roar through the black
a star hangs
over us both

(but if
how approach
these secret
moments)

a bomb burst
light gunfire

the rattle of trucks
over a level crossing

or a more delicate ambush
ends it all.

CLOUD CUCKOO CLOCK

We praise the beauty of these days when everything fits snugly into place and we can see acres of meaning in the sky. Each single realization is dead simple, but inevitably we had forgotten how the suddenness of these perfect moments required a build up: the mulling over of all the possibilities and changes of direction. And while we were looking this way and that, analysing the signs, in the centre of vast continents it was continuing: genocide in the jungle. From our point of view, the world is tidy and principled. Even if you cut off half an arm and a leg, there would be reasons. I no longer focus on normality - in black and white it is always up to me to make the decisions, cropping off the unwanted details. My world is bigger or smaller than yours, depending; but there are moments when the sun tips off the curved edges and is sent spinning in hexagons across the horizon. Again there is a creeping need for power, and you can see it in his smug smile, and the way he acts perfectly controlled at all times. We don't know where those words came from. Thanks to people like us, most of them have disappeared entirely and there can be no dreaming them back, as if out of thin air. Old patches of grammar do survive though, pushing up green through the burnt forest clearings. It's surprising what hope can do to people. At the end of the corridor, beyond mechanical glass doors that slide, hiss and clunk, the prisoners wait, heads down, eyes shifting to and fro. Shrieks cut the air over and over again: 'I told you so! I told you so!' Who is on death row now? It's a pity, but there it is: we are all implicated. If I were you I'd try to forget the pain that is always there, waiting in the wings. The cost of numbers is rising every minute, and the measurement of truth always seems to be changing. The city bars fill up with journalists. Suddenly we are all news, with the cameras selecting our price as we stare at them, dumbfounded. 'Only just over there señor if you would come and look' but they don't understand and have already got back into the taxi. My dreams were of gardens in the clouds, the subtle changes of seasons and all the colours growing and dying, a science of painting with trees, petals, lakes and the percentage of sunlight. It is more difficult than I thought to keep a grasp on it all.

MIDWINTER

Wars balance
on this instant of red space and cold:
we glare into midwinter,
this frozen meeting of eyes.
Only iced black branches hold us apart.

The wedding was in autumn.
Leaves spiralled, confetti
down from the sky,
butterflies dying from summer to snow.
Bells clanged,
the air filled with colour
and time passing.

Now we must choose:
sound or silence.
The distances spin.
Out there are no words,
no clocks.

SNOW POEM

I forget words.
Sometimes there are one,
two, three, and
we spin off the road into a plane tree.
Blood on the snow,
wreck of metal.
At moments like this
you just watch yourself
and think too late
if only   can I
are you   ?
The words are still there
but numb.
The operation is painless.

ALMOST

Almost   in the back of your mind
see things that are there   not quite

and yet
from speculation
to profound analysis

give this flower
one more chance

THEN EVERYTHING WENT BLANK

Green patterns
my mind
the eye
sees what
it will:
flicker of sunbeams
through trees onto
damp shade
where secret flowers
bloom if you will
only look

to capture a moment
(the trick of light
on leaf
as   lemurs leap
from branch
to branch)

and all thoughts such as

high ridges	running down	between the rocks
in mist	the middle	above the surf
blue glimpses	of the poem	on a cold
beyond	to the sea	exposed beach

rhythms of bare feet on wood
the bridge sways
I look up and there
the track leads away across the mountain
into the cloud

cloth slaps on stone
sunlight on wavelap
the riverbanks
spread with colours to dry
and the women wait, chat, sing

their songs elegant as ships sailing unknown to themselves
across a perfect picture
seen from the clifftop in high summer:
the cornfields patrolled by buzzards and the river pinned by herons
a church snug in the hollow behind the sea

and that forgotten gate. A frequent dream. The lane, overgrown,
which seems to lead nowhere. The history of hedgerows full of birds
from spring to spring and the apple blossom blown every year above
the flocks of sheep. These muddy lanes turning into streams as we
speak and the same scene repeated on each continent, as the women
wait and the sails sink
below the horizon

such small signs
such gestures

he smiled and touched
my hand in passing

(thus hatchets are buried)

on the maps
contours and boundary lines are certainties
their silence is trust, unfolded for anyone to see
but
old jokes suddenly explode
and the mountain roads are rumbling with military

this passion for names
the promise smiling through the lies

a vision we all have of a paradise
we have condemned ourselves to

and now who can advise us?

A QUESTION OF SPACE

Summer is confusing.
Watch the petals unfold,
the passage of colours:
flowers give themselves to the light,
the gardens dazzle

and our days run out as the light gets longer.

The cold stretches from one end of the year to the other.
I lie awake, counting the owls,
follow their phrases,
their sentences swooping from nowhere.
They have adapted to the dark.
Nights are long and clean.
Winter is simple.

DEAD END DRIVE

It is the simple things that should concern us. Nothing to worry about, just questions of light on a hillside, changing with the clouds. Or if there is a rainstorm on the other side of the bay, hiding the lights of the town, how it looks from this window, as I mull over all the nuances of what you have just told me. Very interesting. Somehow, although it is okay to defrost the fridge occasionally, I do not feel like making a complete change in my domestic arrangements, and reality and I seem to rub along fine most of the time. For instance just the other day he was telling me that in English there are no words to rhyme with 'orange' or with 'chimney' which in itself is a useful piece of information. Further to your enquiries, yes I did sleep well, and the fogginess has cleared from my vision. A-OK as the medico said. Where does that leave you though? For instance, does television ever frighten you? Its ability to absorb people for more than one sixth of each day? There *are* people who never watch it I gather. Even in the small hours you can see that ghostly flicker through the neighbours' curtains and I'm never sure whether I shouldn't ring them, just to check. But we are all entitled to a little privacy, even the old man sitting alone on the bench over there, talking at his empty cider bottle. Do kids ever shout at you, call you names? If I'm asking too many questions, please excuse me, but I'm worried about you. We used to have such a good relationship. Lying alone in the dark one does sometimes have the most extraordinary visions of what life could be, if only it were given half a chance. The politician in each of us needs to regulate the chaos all around the place, but the child is not so sure, and keeps on experimenting. If I stuck my finger in *there* what would happen if I couldn't get it out? It's all a big dare - some of us are better at coping with risk than others. Anyway there's nothing much in the newspaper today, and as far as thinking about tomorrow is concerned - well, you know what they say. As the afternoon winds on into dusklight, and the birds sing from their roosts, not even the dogs barking up the driveway opposite could distract me from this conversation. It is all so dependent on what you read, dear, and if you buy the wrong sorts of book, well don't blame me. Nothing like that in the library? Not even the librarian had heard of it? Well I never. Just imagine how it could have started: "As the afternoon made the inevitable decision to linger no more, and to change into a definite evening mode, with the varied hues of sea and sky that this usually implies, the Duchess looked around her, and decided it was time for tea." Not that we expect that tone any longer. Now everyone goes for something much more robust. The misuse of language is probably the greatest crime of all, for without saying what you mean you cannot possibly mean what you say. Always distrust the words, even if they are beautifully punctuated. Look at the bar lines, the number of beats, the way the harmonies are resolved toward the end of the phrase. Neat. It's curiously liberating to reach the end of the road, I always find. Turn off the engine, check both mirrors, and open the door. I'll let you off here if that's all right with you. Far off at the corner there is a flash of light, and the smashing of glass. Suddenly the crowd is surging down the street out of control. Sirens. Screams. The thud of heavy boots. Then a ghastly silence as you pick yourself up and try desperately to find something to say, but you find you are in a different time zone and all the systems have changed. Local customs vary. It might be advisable to check with the Information Bureau first, before you go. Perhaps we should not be here at all. There are no maps available. From now on you're on your own. Try talking to the passers by, maybe they will understand you better if you speak up. And always, always remember to smile. Gradually the situation becomes a little clearer, and the sun comes up again to show much the same kind of landscape as the day before, as if you have not moved at all. Oceans of grass billowing in the wind, the occasional horseman trotting across your field of vision, going from one place to another. You wave, and he waves back, which is a start. Even through glass, across such vast distances, there is the possibility of translating dreams into facts, and a careful analysis will show that any preconceptions you had on setting out have been proved false. The water does not taste the same, and neither does the oil, but how many of the vegetables you have eaten have been unrecognizable? Someone can always name them, by taste and smell even if their shape and colour are not always what you expected. Choose three items from the menu, at random if you wish, and the chances are that you will like two of the dishes and besides it gets kind of boring always eating on your own at home. Looking back at the distances they had covered he noted with satisfaction that the village they had left that morning was still there, perched on top of the ridge, glowing in the evening light. Everything was in its place. That evening they celebrated, drinking a bottle of wine round the fire, and singing all the old songs, until the rain started and forced them under cover. No question about it, it had been one of the most rewarding experiences of his life, yet at the back of his mind was still that nagging doubt about how to get back home. He slept fitfully, and when he woke the landscape was covered in thick fog. Every moment being potentially the last, one is well advised to be on one's best behaviour all the time. Are you ready? Then let's go. It isn't what most people would have expected, is it, but we've managed to get used to it. No, there are no buses. They stopped years ago after the riots started. Over there, see? Oh, He's gone. We'll probably see another if we're lucky. Try watching the windows on the upper storeys, that's where they usually are. Over here. Mind your step. Now we really are in the centre of it all. It's a historic spot. Imagine the square filled with tens of thousands of people, all chanting at once, in unison. You've seen the old newsreels? Yes. So here we are. Where it all started. Yes, you may take photos. If you wish.

LIGHT PLAYS

Light plays, keeps its secrets
however long you look.
On another day it may become clear
why, hesitating, the sun in your hair
then the stream to cross:
bells of water jangling
the roar of trees in the wind
all those boulders   lichen on stones
as you summoned up the courage
it is clearer now
but must be   it is   attempted
the bracken is turning
and far off   on the point of
a dog barking
while the clouds   where
less important than when
it graces the fells with bright patches
dancing   there
in front of you

ICE FORMS ON YOUR BREATH

Look at this painting
one of the best of its kind
examine the brushwork
consider the difference between concepts
and their realization

    mist floats between

pines float up from the rock

        here

   you can see

           it is

      there

not painted
a cloudscape with peaks
scattered in the dusk
indifferent to the dying light

Nothing more to say.

QU YUAN

Your face is a long scroll
2,000 years printed on silk
every sound a new meaning
and shapes that change
oh   when asleep   your words
dreaming of water
always whirling   the rain
streaming off the grey roof of this world
down the brown rivers
through the skin
circling the moment   now   when
gong bash and drum
splash of paddles
find the poet
hear the rhythm of his brushstrokes
written on water.

Qu Yuan drowned himself in Meilo River, Hunan, in 295 B.C. His death
is commemorated in the annual Dragon Boat races.

LOTUS STIRRED BY THE BREEZE AT THE DISTILLERY:

AN AUGUST EVENING IN HANGZHOU.

I choose a few words that I think will do nicely,
all colours and shapes,
pack them up to send home to her.
Rich lotus pink. Will she understand
these elegant words in embroidered silk,
or would she prefer something simple and short?
There are so many sounds, long summer days
reading by a lake in the shade,
or smells of hot spices. Far off,
a train rumbles through the mountains, or a distant
taste returns to your tongue. Sweet evening air.
You try to remember,
we speak clearly,
but hear different things:
the intonations of wind among trees or the drone
of traffic through hotel curtains,
morning light rocking the ceiling
or the clanking of plumbing.

There is a word which shall fit you, suit you exactly,
I can find it.
And somewhere in your sleepless journeys there must be
one word for me.
Even a cry or a shake of your head
would be enough.
Fading light on the water. Just a glance.
No, I must reach for my pen and start
forming another letter.
Words have failed us.

THE BRONZE FLYING HORSE, WU WEI, 2nd CENTURY A.D. (LANZHOU MUSEUM)

Green horse I heard you
on the horizon
whirlwind and thunder over the hills
world's end or daybreak gallop above us
slow motion gliding riderless steed
confusing the breezes rival of swallows
high flying master of clouds.

MEETING THE BUDDHA

If you come face to face with him
in the woods on the edge of the cliff,
stare into his unblinking eyes:
you will see out beyond
the far mountains,
listen to the rivers swirling
below your feet, wonder
how long you will wait
before crumbling back into
water and trees.
Hear the plants
growing in your ears,
down your cheek
a long tear of rain
staining the rock.

FOUNTAINS

The invisible church
arches from ruins into sky,
the indivisible light.
It is simple: stone against air
and stone against water,
reflecting the geometries
of power and faith.

It is to withold information
(to not tell the truth)
as it itches behind your eyes,
to achieve this balance
between joy and sadness,
whatever the stone,
whatever the light.

ABSTRACT LIGHT

Watch frost appear at the edge of air,
at the tips of fingers of flame
extending the air into gold.
Day will be night
and all morning shrouded
in cobwebs of cold.
But as this light fades, colours change,
give way. Dawn steams from the field.

As the sunrise
light burns from within the leaf,
shadows are cast upward; the leaves blaze in ice,
fall.
Each leaf speaks its own darkness.

From the flower to this abstract light,
a growth from summer to ice.
Everything has its price:
the light, the leaf.

HIDE AND SEEK

We sit round the silence
listening to space, concentrating;
our thoughts circle the quiet centre of the room.
A faint movement,
far within the darkness, a cry:
there, in the pile of books ?
or in the vase of flowers ?
the sun's flash on a gull, high over the sea.
Light fills the room, floods,
dries again. The far passage of clouds
beyond what the mind cannot grasp,
slipping, losing control.
Nothing will come of it.

To tackle the problem
(heartbeat, itch, uncomfortable chair)
just close your mind and wait,
the clock ticks on,
for the end.
Look up
and there
at the centre, between us all
in a glint of sunlight
the tear drops on the vase.

Weigh the glint of a petal,
measure the patter of rain.

Detailed perceptions
are sudden and mind gold,
mathematical, balanced.

Everything must be written once
then twice with the same words -
new meanings push up, unfold, bloom:
light drips from the roses.

Your thoughts
seeing your profile against the sun
too late
hesitate

WEATHER

On the map
lines veer and back;
black figures indicate
changes in pressure,
the rising and falling
continuities of air.
Our room is set
at a constant 20°.
We can only try to read
what's happening outside,
listen for the thunder
that rolls silent
between the lines.

RECORDED FORECAST

Patterns of weather
are voiced down the phone.
I take note, and watch the sky.

But try to forecast your mood
the quiet terrors of a wet day.

At the end of a long valley
there is no answer
to the unexpected
rain, even.

WAITING FOR WORDS

'As they arrive, send them through.' I try all the days: 1,2,3, some are long and stretch over all the sky. The others creep brownly about the house and nothing gets done. These hot days melt into each other. What poems spin in black orbits, whirring through the infinite silences? What rhymes govern the passage of time, out there where no hand has ever reached for a pen, scrawling desperate attempts to trap the insignificance of it all? Invitations. Promises. Hints. All the words out there somewhere, waiting to make contact. Radio dishes sit in the mist, dripping. Cows munch over the hedge. Impenetrable blank sky. Barbed wire. Each time we hurtle up the road the atmosphere is smashed into fragments, networks of air currents spin behind us, unseen crashes. It is all so closely timed, a sequence of near misses and bits of sound. But we are protected on all sides by glass - lights flash, sun glints, a glimpse of a dead hedgehog, towns on the skyline, as Birmingham gives way to London to Dover and ships swinging with the tide towards shore or horizon in the sinking evening. Small coasters dwarfed by the cliffs encircling the bay. Currents of darkness chill the air. Everything is predictable by rule and book, the Admiralty charts are correct. Although we cannot see it, the reliable sun rises and falls like everything else. Home is now a long way off. Histories and cultures clash in this street where I eat a solitary lunch while waiting for a bus. The square is full of pigeons, I examine all the details: a window ledge, a classical archway. So long ago, oh, an old tune hums and fades as I pick up a newspaper. The dark silence of the early mornings keeps me awake, unless it is the street ringing with drunken footsteps, shouts, and snatches of song. I dream sometimes of highways climbing and swinging over the hills. 'An integral part of the European experience is driving at speed along good roads at night.' Reading the signs, relishing the good maps, enjoying the prospect of a good dinner in a comfortable hotel. The guide books were always right - trust the ads, smile, enjoy... from these deep woods of holiday where no one can reach me, I watch the world waking. Peeled bark hangs off the trees, the white trunks glow in the sun against a polarized blue sky. My wide angle lens catches the thundering arc of white water above us, the battle of verticals as red cliffs and green fans of fern loom over the trail. All these distant memories. Rooms out of focus in the early sunlight, blurred colours through the pane, flowers in the rain. In the old club, the ghosts of gentlemen snore, dreaming of long evenings by the river, the hoot of ships across long oceans of journeys, the traffic of barge up and down, watersplash, nightfall, shadows in the dark lanes where scents of spice and gleams of knife welcome you alone into the centre of the great city. Footprints in the greasy dust on the stairs. The letters criss-crossing. The systems breaking down. Tempers fray, temperatures drop. The sun smears out into drizzle, the ache of grey skies, wastes of wind over the lakes, bare trees, drab fields across the plain. How many poems travel out there, jolting along the tracks, lost in the cold dusk, collapsing for want of a sense of direction?

JUST A MOMENT

The room seems quite still

A bubble at the rim of a glass of water
bursts

A pool of light on the carpet
fills and dries as clouds pass
in their far silence

A flower dies in its vase

Dust falls

Do not move, even this gently
Do not move your eyes

your fading sight is disturbing

OLD POET

The centuries of paper shift, pile up.
He holds a poem to the light
to see its watermark.
Can I see through it?
Leaves it out in the sun
for pages to curl and crack,
yellow till the print fades,
or leaves it under the rain
to see if the ink runs.
The unwritten poems line his shelf
stiff in a military authority,
bright in smart jackets.
Cracked limestone face,
clothes covered in ash,
he shuffles around, coughing,
tasting time; a frayed
illegible knowledge.

MAPS

Each time I look I see
a quicker way to go
yet those alleys and back streets
are secret! for all the world
I would not tell anyone
about that day I saw

the maps reveal nothing.
They hang on the wall,
inner problems exposed:
London, Paris.

SUMMER FUNERAL

Images float up through the red light,
grandparents, my father.
No amount of water can wash it off,
my hands stink of fixer.
Swallows twitch on the wire, waiting to go,
the nights are tightening,
flowers pressed dark between pages,
but there is as much time left as before;
bread smells from the oven, the first winter soups.
Each photo is numbered.

THE VIEW FROM THERE

I watch my mother go
helpless
she floats just out of reach

staring down at us all
speechless
the sad look in her eyes

CARTOGRAPHIES

I

We create our own cities
in the sad spaces of the heart

for true orange is one of the colours of silence
and whenever you sense that hint of winter on a foreign day
you trust to memory

as: iron grilles along a whitewashed wall
sounds of fountains hidden from the long road
the scattered street sounds ripple through shade trees

the tang of joy
coming alive with this beauty
then reckoning the price
making time

(at all costs protect the workings of the heart:
'the thirsty man is the last to drink')

there is no shortage
of work to be done
but no one
to pay for it

cracked bells

echoes

II

Jagged edge, black etched on blue night, silhouette against stars.
The death of a year in ice.

This north wall has never known the sun, cold rock cuts us off
from the south; those mountains are gold, at early hours they stand
up high into the pale air.

After weeks, the steel unlocks.
Thick fog weighs on the hills, the farms
float in and out of white darkness
waiting, the trees in patterns of glass
drips of light
breath of silence on rock.

First seen a hundred miles off, painted on sky, a hint of spring as the
road climbs and falls. A thin line on the horizon, imagined snow
through the trees, love slowly taking shape.

He remembers the tones of salads,
notes the structures of lettuce,
and eats slowly.

Every night in a new hotel
but no favourite,
every one his own.

'A palace of air... the King ...
This time I must get it right.'
he moves forward uncertainly

'A water garden...'
- What about your job?
- This won't hurt at all...

It is a small house in which he stands.
Each blade of grass, each broken shell
is minutely depicted, he calls it
the Kingdom of the Soul:
just feathers, leaves, things that drift.
A vision that recurs,
a Chinese garden of cork
carved in a glass case.
How many countries are behind his eyes?

The week begins with the bells,
the cathedral booms
and our street echoes with its bass drone,
treble peal up over the roofs.
A figure on the stairs,
do you know her name?
She sings a long song without words. At the end is a mirror. She
stops dancing. Her hands are like marble, perfectly still. At a glance
she could destroy all song. Look into the glass.

At the back of the sky
the sea thunders
behind the trees

The forest is quiet
a few birds silenced
by the ocean's roar

The march of pines through the night, black trunks against the blue
light of dawn. Change trains at the border. The moon rises from
behind a hill, sets again as the train moves on. The lights of a far
town shift in the dark. We enter a new past, as bridges lean to adjust
their angles to our line of flight. Moon sits in the window, blinking
between trees, through darkness and patches of mist. A war is
brewing beyond the horizon, early morning thunderstorms, strange
breakfasts.

III

The dancing blue-green fountain of light reflects
swirls of tiles and immaculate stone lacework,
the plaster Koran's mathematical play
marching strict round the walls,
the dark designs of cedar and bronze.
Every angle is patterned with Allah,
water and quiet. A paradise
for intellect and prayer.

Outside
the sun
filters through to a chaos
of alleys
donkeys and children
splash of mud
scarred faces smiling
secret eyes glint of gold
the air clanging
spices burnt meat and cedar

The city
is on the edge of centuries, a dry sea.
Mud palaces stand over dazzling sands.
Midsummer hours burn into years
of rock and dead armies.
Sun sculpted stones litter the hills.
Spring is a thousand miles away.

(True orange
is a quality of light,
the sweet dew of dawn,
perfumed with flowers,
the laced play of water on carved columns.
Deep sky and red earth,
a ghost of heat
on the tongue)

IV

Cracked bells clang at random
punctuate the dark

dog barking at its own echo
down a backstreet

trust memory for all you need

and so we create our own sad cities

for silence is one of the colours of winter

and no fountains play behind the grille

the sounds of joy hidden from the long street

the costs reckoned
the time marked

protect us from the workings of echoes

no shortage of work

cracked bells
bark

that thirst again

THE LOST ORNITHOLOGIST

Without a field guide, the ornithologist is lost.
All the new birds to recognize... thousands
of features. How, adequately, to describe this
in terms of that? The absence of sound:
no rustles of paper here, just the movement of waves
and flitting shadows. He gives himself time
to wonder, inspecting the lenses,
polishing with a soft cloth. A starting point,
knowing the landscape so intimately, and
avoiding the clutter of observable detail,
to ponder the value of the abstract:
clouds in the mind, the patterns of gulls,
noon light on water seen from a clifftop,
and so many changes - each leaf, each rock
an individual. These limitations, and
these strengths. With fieldglasses
he can see for miles.

HERE

This is the quiet place
just before dawn.

All night the cold air has been rolling
down from the hills.
As winter moves in we get closer,

recollect what it was.
The empty house is very calm now.
Just the two of us
barely needing to communicate.

We wake early
deprive ourselves of sleep
for such moments:

the glare of gold behind the trees,
fan-shaped patterns of black on the skyline.
Love is always surprising me:

yesterday
just before dusk
the rainbow spanned our world from end to end.

The sky was another valley.

COMMUNICATIONS

A few scratches on a shell
scuffs of sand on a worn stone

they shout at us across the centuries

but how to articulate this sudden sorrow

the same room
the same light swaying
through the curtains

where my mother died

the sadness comes at me
sudden on still afternoons
out of empty sleep

how to articulate all these images
which won't go away?

from the same room
where my mother

staring back across the room
a few photos
a summer afternoon

scratches winking on glass
as the daylight changes

a few letters

voices

you smile
uncomplaining
face bruised by sleep

and at the end of your road
a light winks from the sea.

SO NEAR

That crazy gleam in your eye
the same old smile
after all these years
I watched you run down the beach into
and another beach somersaults four or
five
a few photos
were there
were you laughing
I nearly

SITTING IN YOUR ROOM

Giving, taking,
what is the difference?

Your white room is just right.
A happy poster smiles at the morning
light reading the bright titles along the shelves.
Your plants breathe in a new air.

Blobs and patches jump round the walls
where I stared too long at the sun.

Do thoughts meet here:
the empty glass on the table
the half game of chess
waiting for me to play?

All our words are duets now.

FIDELITY

Just lying here with my eyes closed
I can see some lovely things.

In daylight there is even more:
people smile at me, welcoming
the promise in casual encounters

I roll over and put my arms round you
sleeping sound

testing with my mind
the physical limits of the world.

SONG ?

The shattering dream
all last night
shared with you
I must reconstruct

is it an ache
for

trying to reconstruct
(from memory? words?)
our shattering dream.
I woke. I returned to her
and we continued
as we fell back to sleep.
Remember   the way
she looked
                    and
        in the light

or was it an ache
I listen for
not so much meaning
or any specific phrase
but the catch in your voice

when we read poems
as evening burns on into candlelight
is it an ache for someone
I listen for
not so much meaning
as the way you

but the catch in your voice
at the back of my mind
a perfection we only can
sometimes
glimpse
a catch of

EXPLORATIONS

Barely awake in this strange room
through your windows I heard
duets of robins across the valley
and the woodpecker's drum rattle
in the early light through cold twigs
beyond where the river rose and fell
on its way to the end of the bed,
and in dreams sometimes I still see
how you came to me that first time
across a wide ocean,

how your ships left these misted hills
and disappeared years beyond our horizons
creeping south within sight
of palm-forested surf, circling the coasts,
hugging Africa, making landfalls
on imagined continents, recording their customs
and naming their mountains higher than clouds
(as if words matter at all)
and as you come you cry out once more
waving farewell.

PLEASE

You must see the dawn
even if only to catch sight of

and beyond the hill
with the birds singing

the appalling clouds
wiping out all

as we wake and make coffee
staring out of the front door
at the gloomy garden

it rained all night
I could not
you kept turning over and
it was my fault
you said you didn't

and if we can't catch sight
just for a moment

BACK BEARINGS

That dream of boats
the swinging tides
and unforeseen windshifts

an anguish of
half-remembered trysts
and love-long afternoons
on the cliffs

then the weather changed:
the black hills of clouds
with vivid green storms
hitting the coast

(but memories trick,
we fail to understand
first time and so
relive the pain -

how many times have we watched
the fleet sail out
beyond the breakwater
into the night?)

red green white
clear sectors
blinking through the spray

pilotage:
tricks of the current,
leading lines

TWO VERSIONS

(Looking at scroll paintings in Shanghai museum)

Quiet mornings looking at silk scrolls
unrolled through the memory of previous mornings
by lakes where old men stare into blank water for fish,
not a ripple disturbing the old fabric but
a permanent bird's eye view of
sweeps, loops, swirls of ink,
fine lines without perspective,
blossom   mists   mountains floating
over the edge of the silk
clouds
a silken beauty gazes at the fish
as a bullock cart rumbles down the lane,
a peasant limps behind, barefoot, whip in hand,
cursing
fine lines without perspective.
The beauty stares into the blank water
as the cart rumbles away
blossom   mists   mountains fading
at the edge of her tattered silk

CARNIVAL

Boom of trombones, the heavy drummed thud
of a death-march rhythm,
the slow steady creak of feet on snow.
Masks grin from the flickering shadows
of carved wood in torchlight,
silent faces from the panelled rooms
stare out at the same unchanging view:
forest, the strong houses, the deep winter street.
A quiet people; their carnival.

WATCHING FOR GOLD

What draws me to these coasts?
Lizard, the Dodman. I dream
in washes of grey.
Where do these songs come from?

Syncopations of light,
an abstraction from the real
to the essence of what could be
an architecture of the mind.

How the eye follows
each curve and twist
providing images out there
in the mist.

Deceptive shapes,
but enough signs,
enough warnings:
hints of ships.

Learn, then just as easily
forget. Numbers come
and go, annual subtractions
till I reach zero.

So many steps
between me and the words.
So many interesting things
and all within reach

but

analyze the sweep of light
on the swell of the waves
in the evening ocean,

the way the west moves
into darkness and the roar
of the stones in the surf.

THE GOODNIGHT KISS

The sea is calm after the storm swell,
fine high skies again.

Tensions of weather, of air,
the dance of words through the night.

How the personal and the political intermingle:
TV, radio, papers...

are these questions worth asking
when the answers are there in front of you?

(The flowers, the butterflies
in the afternoon sunlight).

A distinction between the world of rhymes
and the poem as air, lighter, more interesting

ah...my dreams are true to form:
a goodnight kiss.

The difficulty is to keep all this
in the palm of your hand,
knowing it may all blow away,

continuing your reading
consulting your dictionary
expanding your vocabulary.

Anxieties of form:
the difference between the words you need
and the words you use

(no way of telling what will appear,
or more important, what it will mean
in the end).

Sorting out all the old papers,
the paragraphs and comments,
the ripped pages

the sounds are gone,
meanings without feeling:
a noise of words but no content.

Caught in the crossfire
keep your head down and keep thinking

matching the imagination to all its possibilities...

AND THEN

Following logic to its ultimate patterns
the sun will inevitably
    because the smile is such that
no reason is needed
    and there is always a danger
of erring into silence
    the veering towards chaos
(that is an access to truth)

    shout   dance   sing
and all the new snow on the mountains
    as the sky clears to a morning blue
so much closer than yesterday

    who is responsible   who do you think
you cannot make accusations without proof

    watch these spaces very carefully

PROBLEMS IN THE OVERFLOW CARPARK

(or ETHNIC CLEANSING *versus* TOTAL QUALITY MANAGEMENT)

I

And they came
not in the order we had expected,
but singly, or in hundreds,
or in pairs and in families,
alighting here or there on branches,
chairs, a curtain rail, or on the stairs,
and sat there conversing among themselves,
or staring blankly into space
with a look of shock, as if the outside world
had decided, by a cursed magic, to change their race,
and still they kept on arriving, ghosts of themselves,
their previous lives still evident
there in a sweep of hair or a gesture of hands
reminiscent of elves
or in a manner of blinking
to stop themselves cry
as if to say:
"I was there, I was there, you cannot understand
                           however
hard you try
and I do not need your emotional blackmail
just give me the basics and the time
to dream my freedom back."

When silence fell
at dusk
when without more fuss
they rolled on their sides
and slept
I understood they were here to stay
and once back home, I wept.

By the way the stream roared all night
I knew there were many questions without answers

By the way the stars pierced the wisps of cloud
I knew some answers are always inexplicable

By the way the steam rose again from the fields at dawn
I knew this was only one possibility among thousands

By the way the birds sing earlier and earlier these
                                        mornings
I knew the years' turning is inevitable

You can keep your love safe in a little black bag
and open it on special occasions
like a treat to offer at weekends.
But what if

Those elegant patterns of light and shade,
transient but recurring. These forms of words,
those careful phrasings

II

When not to hurry   signifies
a hidden agenda

(that's what
you've always been thinking)

so that between the trees, having inserted the coin
pushed the red button
and waited, faintly amused by the process,
for the neatly-printed ticket
confirming today's date and the time of this exact moment
(hours minutes and seconds in Eastern Standard,
or Mountain, or GMT, or UST, or dammit
in forget-me-not blue and dandelion clock time?)

reminded yet again of the moment
you stroll back to the car
and between the trees catch a

now that tune again, from *Oklahoma*?
or was it *Free as Air*
I heard it just then,
something to do with the breeze
and the lake water lapping between
the young leaves

but then I smelt compromise
and the gestation of terrors

That's it! THE REASON FOR THIS CONFUSION,
FOR THE HESITATION IN PUTTING DOWN
EXACTLY
WHERE THIS THOUGHT COMES FROM!

I was strolling back to the car, having paid
for a two-hour parking ticket,
and I was reaching in my top pocket for the key
so I could prop the card on the dash

just like any other law-abiding driver
when I caught a catch
between the trees
of light off the lake and

now the day has faded
and my head is clear
I can finally settle and start
to think what it was all about

The lake light through the leaves
the reflections of sunlight
through green spring.
A hope for something we've forgotten.
A promise. Some hope.

A glimpse of the rose tinted peaks
as the shutters ajar let a breath
of fresh morning into the stale room

the good dreams ate the stones
digested the shrapnel,
the sharp bits

Let go the finite
let it run its course
the day to day
the routine
let it settle its own affairs

The possibilities
need consideration
the once in a lifetime
the sudden
seize it with both hands and run!

Down the sky to its limits
these dark green hillsides
dripping with drizzle.

III

THE promise of rain
the absence of light
the manipulations of mist
the tissue of lies
the cobwebs of time
the dusts of absence
the light of dark
the moon of day
the stars of noon
the gleam of hope
the grin of despair
the ravine
the valley
the flag
the menace of laughter
the smell of fear
the forced march
the departures at dawn
the helmets
the plans and maps
the letter marked "Return to Sender"
the fax
the old chest
the medal
the fallen petals
the enigma of words
the six legged dog
the black flag
the alarm
the scent of clouds
the movement of rock
the dream of rivers
the closed door
the red bucket
the rubber ball

the desert
the snowpeaks

the cloudscapes

THE HALFWAY

Then it clouded over.
We didn't care
what had happened before:
'this is it.'

Balance the effect against the intention,
the purpose against the truths of desire,
make attempts to hold those old visions
clearly against the onset of winter
(did you hear the hail against the pane?)

On the table my half-empty glass
fills with flamelight which grows
as the room darkens and darkens.
I tiptoe around, skirting problems,
brushing against secrets, hoping
the candle will not die as I carefully
turn the handle and let the door swing
open on its fine old hinges.

By subdividing past truths
into ideal and abstract moments,
this phase of light
when birdsong becomes silence
can go either way:
day into dusk into darkness,
or through dawn into daylight again.

WHERE TO GO AFTER THIS

Replace passion
with a promise

or lust
with love

the dream
with reality

fictions
with fact

these adjectives
with a noun

and the indefinite
with definite articles.

Tell one lie
to think 1000

starve a truth
to feed deception

say yes
and cause a crisis

(blink an eyelid
start a war

sign the papers
start a fire)

say no
to reinvent innocence
on the edge of the possible:

crystal bowls of fruit
behind locked glass,
these cupboards
of domestic secrets.

UNSETTLED DEBTS

Other people's words too
much in my head

we need our own talk
our own music
the smell of silence
and drip of rain
from your window
(lagoons of weekend
calm
beyond which
the crashing week
cannot reach us)

I read late
to remind myself
of the ocean swell

those magnificent sunsets

and now between these hills
a rainbow
tells us of weathers
and continual change beyond our garden
the sun sparkle on dew:
worth a photo, no?

so back to work
plotting
imagining names
measuring distances
from here
to here

(the crises
in other countries
all now

explained

to our own satisfaction)

WALKING IN THE GARDEN

On the balcony of an old hotel, surveying the sea.
The flickering images die with the light
and the sound of a forgotten script echoes
somewhere over the horizon, beyond where
in a backstreet, or by a river, under a lamp
50 shadows are waiting by a parked truck.

TV's monopoly on silence.

A horse trotting down the lane into dawn
or the rattle of metal on stone,
or the tumbling of branches on the skyline.
And perhaps a high gale-torn sky
with planes and helicopters criss-crossing,
and hardy petals still clinging
in the lee of a wall:
winter, and the crunch of first frost underfoot
(smashing of glass! the flicker of orange on the screen
and the delight of those faces in close up!)

What to do but wait, look again at your watch,
pace up and down the balcony,
decide not to leave until

you have seen the idea itself, pure and sparkling,
like the early light gliding over the hilltops
and the serene glow of the sky.

Westerlies pouring in -
storms of birds hurtling over the hill
and rain on the air.

At the end of the long light
as the shadows thicken
and a late bird flits black,
you hear a tune, or a memory
of a walk long ago in a garden
when, holding your hand, she patiently
pointed out all the items of interest:
out there beyond the wall
small silences between the trees
the grasses waiting

a laugh beneath the pond

a cloud in full flight
cancels the light

walking stops.

MATCHINGS

We intrude on this wedding of earth and sky:
a theoretical landscape too vast for us to dream,
where ideas are toys (politics or their local equivalent).
Lark song over bracken, the deep blue stretching,
stretching

and we will become secrets of stones,
of tortoiseshell glimmers of mystery in brown,
and the sudden flash of sapphire through a tree
when, surprised by parakeets

but what liberation
as we doze, or swim in the warmth
under a hazy sky on some expensive island

is it
or no

UH-OH!

When the late light
  fingers the trees
and the haze deepens
  to a murk
of misunderstood shapes and fears
and the long dark enters
the yard

then

reach for the phone
and softly dial
home

before the gates
close?

ATTENTION! UN TRAIN PEUT EN CACHER UN AUTRE

So all it needs then is for the spies
(who would otherwise have returned home)
to keep on working. And the mountains,
which are so near in this high blue, will
as always regard the lake with,
what shall we say, indulgence.
Or will it be differently plotted?
As the borders close, and the papers
pile up, and the dead sentries' families
go their own way (school? or the cellars!)
whose alphabet will matter after all?
In an age without gunfire, eyes closed
or open will not matter. Keep working
towards a brighter future. The fires
die out and another metal gleams.
Crafty, eh? No plans, no maths.

LEARNING TO READ AGAIN

I read differently now, and my writing has changed:
words drift off the page (or is it my eyes?)
and where I say 'a' the sense goes 'uh'.
The sentences hesitate as if they were saying
'something else lurks behind these pages -
you have picked the wrong book. Turn back to page one.'

So I start to translate, working one speech into another,
and attempting new scripts. There, no alphabet
but a structure of bars to prevent thieves from entry -
like iron grilles on dark windows in unlit backstreets
where foreigners are not welcome. There, no language
but strange mathematics waiting for proofs.

QUIET QUESTIONS

The facts pile up. We do nothing but think and think, staring below us out of the window at the clouds. No talking! In the showcase beyond the photocopier and the reference books, all the fruits of paradise were displayed behind glass, lit by a magnificent sunrise. Mango, papaya, the very names made me drool with desire, and I dreamed: wandering here and there through old scraps of notes, I read names of mountains, rivers, deserts, lakes, villages, trees. The old cities of the dry plain have been blown to dust, but the mud-bricks are catalogued, like the birds that circle the ruins at evening. All you can carry, from season to season, are these memories and ideas. We rewrite history to suit our changing interpretations of pasts seen from presents and a continually unrolling future, which we glimpse far off as the highway climbs and swoops and curves through the night. We cross vast distances where the only radio contacts are chat shows through the dark drizzle. Fasten seat belts. Extinguish cigarettes. Below us, in the heat of the night, the Red Sea, sunrise over the Indian Ocean, the storm clouds piling up over the horizon, and now

ACHIEVEMENT INDICATORS

These gentle qualities of northern light
endless moments of slow falling evening
dripping from the leaves and rocks, but
their grey minds and restless hearts

and so the tang of tar on the mist
chattering birdsong, far swash of waves on the sandbanks,
moorings, departures, and we did not grasp
the meanings of these creaking ropes and timbers

then blues from across the forest, swamp sounds
on the edge, a breath of desert sometimes in their faces,
short dusks and instant sunsets
into tropical darkness and nightsounds

the horror the tears the nightmares of blood
the pain of witness, of hearing
ripped skin and smashed bone
with the slash of machetes through screams

and laughter spicing this picnic of death
and the flies the flies in the empty eyes

their weather all gone wrong, forever

ALL THOSE BICYCLES

Gradually, we take less care.
Rust creeps along the joints,
threads wear. The shining black
paint is chipped.

Over the tannoys
they broadcast the trial
of 80 young criminals.
One city alone:
all are shot.

Everyone is wearing uniform
winter jackets.

It gets light
later and later.
Moon festival soon.

FREEDOM FIGHTERS

What are the contexts of pain then? In which land do sufferings increase, where decrease, and where can one make the most of one's leisure? On what scale does one measure societal pressures? I dream of coasts, of seaswell strangely shrouded in mist, and as the heat haze disperses I see a row of breakers, with a thin green line of palms. Huts, long painted boats, sunbathers, the boys waiting in the shade. Remember what you can, while you can. There is no going back now the journey has started. Someone said 'You never return to where you set out from.' There is no coming back. You yourself have changed. And it's not just a question of getting the words down, onto paper. It is the organizing principle, the thought that counts, weighs, measures.

By golly he takes himself seriously! Be aware of each named place: its mark on the pattern: Chilly Bridge, Bridge of Gore, York, Yes Tor, Leicester, Cirencester, Westerham, Hampton Court, Portsmouth, Watersmeet, Bridgewater, Ironbridge... the words travel from hill to hill, down the valleys, around woods, in all weathers. They can be understood only by walking, or on maps with great care, seated under a lamp at night, when the mind can go rambling (even the lanes are choked with surprises!) Making the most of every moment, I see in the patterns of light at the end of the lane a distant disturbance of dust, and a noise coming from over the hill towards the combe. As the car passes the distant cyclist waves, and the clouds move on in their stately progress towards other places. The house martins are still fidgeting in and out of their nests under the eaves, and the swallows twitch on the telegraph wires, waiting to go. Sudden collusions of natural forces can take us by surprise. Who would have thought that the earthquake on the other side of the globe would affect the rain patterns here? But really it's obvious, isn't it, when it has happened everyone happily accepts it as common knowledge. But two weeks ago the same people thought you were mad, my dear, there there. The sun hesitates, and goes back to sleep behind its clouds. Stay inside then, keep out of the damp. Your chest, there, make sure it's well-covered. We rented a car and went over the moor. Who's teasing, then? He sits there all day and never says anything. And he used to be such a fine figure of a man. Lord, you should have seen us! We did lead them a dance! How we laughed! Plug in the kettle. Switch on. Look in the mirror. First, second, gently, third, and away we go. Up to about fifteen thousand it's clear, and then there are side winds and trails of cloud. Birmingham down to starboard, a beautiful sunset to your left. Don't worry, we'll only be thirty minutes or so. The motorways snaking in and out of the pink rippling rooftops, the puddles and sheen of rain on the landscape for miles in each direction. Now, black or white? Sugar? Mind how you go on this bend, leaves and mud, they're building a new road up past the golf course. Have you all got your harnesses? Clips fastened? Ready then, open the hatch. Your first jump in cloud. Don't worry. I'll bring it, don't you get up. Have a look at the TV if you want, I won't be a moment. God, the stairs! He said to come back on Thursday, but how can I when there's no buses? I'll ask if there's a car service.

On and on, as usual. The radio confirms what I thought, No pineapple, no mango ever tasted as good as then - the early morning light filtered through the curtains and you were hard-pressed to remember where you were. Here? And if not, why not? Such answers are required, it will take a lifetime or more to formulate the questions, even with computer enhanced imaging. As Beethoven wrote key changes and chords, which by their very structure reach out for meaning, so we try to interpret those sounds in the context - not of Java or Japan, but of Mozart and Chopin. The instrumentation flickers, according to the century, in Indian ink traced by brass nibs, or rapid laser printing with green lights, or the flutter of prayer flags and the oracle's writhings. In those days crowds would gather from miles around, some had walked for weeks to attend the ceremonies. Zapping from channel to channel we try to determine a scheme but the information we obtain is all contradictory. When the CD machine goes on the blink, what conclusions do we dare draw? Look behind you, no, over there. Did you see what I did? Perhaps it is safer to remain where we are and concentrate on the work in hand, the books and papers that demand our attention. But my gaze keeps wandering and I sense that out there, far below in the city streets, there is an urgency and a bustle unusual for a Sunday afternoon. It is not holiday time, nor is the weather even particularly fine. On the phone you sounded fraught, and I could not tell if anyone else was there. Did you cup your hand over the mouthpiece once, to shout a question up the stairs? How I hope not. As it turned out, while waiting for the coach, the last thing we wanted to talk about was us. We shuffled our feet and rearranged the luggage, and listened to the other people comparing notes on the restaurants. Out in the bay, the racing yachts were like paper flowers unfolding in water, as the spinnakers were shot and the sun glared through the blue breezes of high summer. The policemen were in short sleeves, the flags were waving, and the town was dancing. I waved at the departing coach and walked back to the station where a mass of forms was piled, waiting to be sorted through. A notepad and pen, clear notes in the margins, the tiny handwriting a testimony to a lifetime's neatness. When the phone rings, I ignore it, or turn up the volume on the answering machine to see if I want to respond. A clinical lack of direct contacts, a jangle of percussion, bent notes, senses awry, everything broken down. Yeah.

TRACTS

Reveal
fantasies of history

undo
the work of centuries

study
the secrets of stones

renew
wartimes of bitterness

(remind me
 how they used to deal
     in gestures
handing you a bottle of flower wine
     a jar of jam

the local fruit
symbol of the earth
they stood on

          such pities
          such misunderstandings

spring songs
     in summer
     remembered as autumn gales
   staring into a winter fire
        we sip the year's juice)

destroy
illusions of peace

HELPLINE

Making the most of
these moments of indecision

the weather doesn't help:
hot blue sky day after day

maximum tension must always be maintained
throughout the process at risk of failure

the soil crumbles underfoot
the rain beats on the window

memories of drought and thirst
swollen bellies and pleading eyes

the heating goes on with a clunk
the pipes vibrate through the snoring house

flies buzz in the dark room
fire embers stir, rats scratch

the fax machine has jammed again
and we can only get their bloody answerphone

at the crossroads lights flashing
uniforms controlling the traffic

somewhere over the horizon a plane
droning towards us through the heat

photos remind us but tell others
very little of the facts

we are making every effort
to improve our service to clients

THE MAGICIAN

I can invent facts,
for instance: 'You have red hair.'
This is good enough for my purpose.
To be more detailed
would invite questions.
We all create our own fictions
so do not ask
'Was it yesterday?'
My trousers are striped
and I wear a top hat.

HOW IT COMES TO THIS

To amaze
        make scenes
(almost it seems
        as a matter of course)
        and then just as soon
forget where all that
        came from

as ever it continues
the dance of light
        and our fantasies
(is it only vanity after all?)
        in the fall of her hair

that air of grievance
        pouting over her shoulder

(in the end all just
        a cold dry thing)

how it comes to this
spreading out on the page

picking up the pieces
and letting them fall like
a child's bricks on a carpet
                and refusing to tidy

cough of a pheasant

the erratic perfection
of butterflies across
        the garden

TO START WITH

Not much to go on:

a chill day with long clouds
washing dawn below the horizon.

Only a moment
between mudflat and flood.
The low levels of grass and saltwater
busy with waders,
the air rich with weed.
A gull drifts over on its way elsewhere.

Rigging clinks, a clock in the wind.

Enough time to start with.

ANYTHING COULD HAPPEN

Anything could happen as you gently
without waking the others
step from the bed and move to the kitchen
open a window to breathe in the new day
the stars fading and an ant exploring the sink
undisturbed as you reach for a glass
and turn on the tap
let it all run slowly through your hands
the water   the cool air   the dawn.

REREADING THIS, NOW

When you look back on this day I describe,
the waft of light through the curtains
and rustle of eucalyptus over the terrace
in the dry heat of afternoon,
the lingering satisfaction of coffee, then siesta and sleep,
lying on a couch with the pale blue light
washing the walls, the mirror,
reflecting on your own position as reader
of innumerable other anecdotes about past lives,
can you try, half asleep by the fire perhaps,
or, aperitif on the table beside you
as you gaze out over the bay,
the cool evening breeze stirring the trees,
the far splash of kids in the pool,
and a jet reaching across from our world to the next,
arching over your head as you strain your eyes in the sunlight,
to guess where, of all the places it might be heading,
this is, the starting point?

LINES WAITING FOR A MEANING

Snapshots of weddings and coastlines:
the little known corners of foreign thought

entering a new past, where facts and figures,
the colours of memories,
are mixed on a stranger's palette
with a different set of brushes

and the delicate nuances you once trusted
are now shown up as lies

borders redrawn
stories rewritten
(even your grammar has changed)

for no poem's as important
as this gurgle of breath from the crib
and your wakeful wriggling
in the early light through the curtain

(rain hugs the coast
the cliffs are a quiet darkness
behind the grey:
dawn is a change of mood
but there's no change at all in these rhythms of water)

AT A LIBRARY WINDOW

I read in circles
struggling to follow one man's
strange ideas.

Birds fly overhead;
I watch them to the sky's edge
with weak eyes.

JET LAG

The beach is like a clean page, washed by the tide. Contemplate, lying in the sun, the words that could be written there: the chatter of unseen birds through the trees and the frantic ticking of insects. The turquoise shallows are interrupted here and there by rocks. A slight breeze ruffles your hair, these pages.

Writing on the beach, the problem is to resist rolling over and dozing. Do half-formed words, the lazy rocking of the waves through your head, make ideas, or must they be clearly expressed? Perhaps words are merely tricks of your mind.

This is an attempt to explain, to identify, to classify new information, but what is needed most is a perfect emptiness of thought. The lists, made so laboriously, the piles of paper, get forgotten. After a lifetime, what do these old men think, as they walk on the shore, watching the girls in the surf, and dreaming? Do they want to build their own houses on stilts, overlooking this perfect bay, or sail south, homewards, over the horizon?

There are no secrets. The trees drip flowers, fruit hang in clusters, and the insects are deafening. The play of wind on waves, the words alone, are enough. Close your eyes and swim in this ocean of words.

HEAT HAZE

How loud the silences seem
when you've had enough sun
a cloud's passed across the late afternoon
and the woods are filled with the chatter of birds

a moment
unbearably peaceful
                    and loud
                    with calm
so the only sound is your own
        anxious
            heart

then beyond the river and the road
    leading over the hill to the clouds
        and uncertain sunlight
            before us now

is it

or not
            and why
                then

        whatever

AUTUMN IN THE TEAHOUSE

Rust brown jasmine tea
from a cracked bowl. Plane leaves fall
round the black kettle.

Written at Du Fu's house outside Chengdu.

Something has changed overnight.
The light is different.

The air has been dancing
and now the photograph is quite silent.

Everything is much further away.

The snowman is laughing
because we can't go to school.
We can't even get out of the door.
He has danced round our house.

We'll go skiing tomorrow.
I'll take you to where
there is deep powder snow.

A man walking through the snow
closely followed by two black dogs.

He is going through a quiet period.

I turn my head so slowly that no one realizes
I am a wolf.

TRAINING RUN

Matching the imagination to all its possibilities.
Disease. Error. Chance. The tactics of meetings.
Policy statements. News broadcasts. The handing out
of disinformation. So many rarified conversations
between the Men in Suits and Representatives
of Foreign Powers whose flags you don't recognize.

In the corner, a bearded man in white robes smiles,
putting the finishing touches to his ultimate letter.

Images. Conversations. Snatches of gambits

    emptiness

          the whine of cars below the window

datelines   fear of fire

   stengths of style   real power

          magnification

  analysis in close-up

how the scientists manage, at the end of the day, to particularize
the patterns of existence, create their formulae, graphs, clines,
research the minutiae, calculate the infinite moods of changing
phenomena, bargain for reality with the theoretical and describe
the whims of unknown systems

seems like they are making some kind of a confession, just for us.

    Find the ratio, the balance,
    maybe one in ten?
    (unless it should revert to just another memory
    scents of flowers on a hot day
    or a hint of soap on a clean face...)

Rig the vote. Make an effort to understand. Wait. Write reports.
Interfere with the local systems. All the games we play, life as
ever reflecting sequences of mirrors down a long passageway.

BORDER DISPUTES

Somewhere out there beyond the borders
Where no one would imagine it could happen,

Not a sound in the snows.
A cloud passed in front of the sun.

In the distance, the same solid rock,
A few days' walk at least.

This is the problem of politics.
If it is all only words

Why do these questions keep recurring?

He kept asking, 'My brother,
My brother, where is he?'

But they had all moved away
To another town, years ago.

He was the last of the old men to return,
And no one recognized him.

The uses of logic are frightening,
And the absence of news.

NOT TO MENTION THE WEATHER

The ship will rock, when, much later
you remember the smaller details, as if
under hypnosis or in the fragments of a dream
and the facts you thought forgotten
will probably be much more frightening:
the way she smiled as she waved
goodbye and the plea in the child's eyes
as you handed her one last cent;
the dead trucks wrecked by the roadside
and the litter of panic: odd shoes, broken toys,
a dropped umbrella, and a brand new hat
perched on top of an upturned dustbin.

Too many resonances: the aims of it all
(treaties, borders) are lost in the echoes
of names, battles, defeats and victories,
cries for vengeance and celebrations of power.
Speeches are pasted on trees, or nailed up
to the doors of the great houses; the newsreels
flicker, with scratchy recordings of dead voices.
TV is only just as slick: video replay replaces,
in freeze-frame, the hi tec gore and horror
with the old engraver's art of caricature.
Reality becomes stereotype, a satire of itself.

The clichés thicken and clot our brains.
Sentimental ballads seem to offer liberation,
but are on the black market - a good idea
at the time. The morning after, count the broken
bodies and bottles. Armoured cars whine
down the lanes, the air crackles with static.
Smoke from the four corners. Nowhere to run.
Switch off the TV. The dead men slept
in your living room during the night
and departed, leaving hardly a trace. Not a word.

I have a dream... (or was it a nightmare?)
Then the dead in all the underground cities
will wake up and scream: "We were fooled!"
And the dogs that howl the nights through
will slink away down the forgiving alleys,
and the man in the new hat will scrutinize us
with a half-smile playing on his lip,
and the dawn will be delayed by the dark
storm blocking the mouth of the harbour.

A MILITARY EXERCISE

We sit and listen to the radio, pondering the impossible:
the tourists don't come any more.
How could they, with the fires and alarms
along all the borders?
One boat still rocks in the bay,
the last old captain listens to jazz
all day in his hut by the shore.
The wind carries rumours, there is smoke
in the air, and helicopters clatter overhead
to their targets up in the hills.
The electricity, of course, was always erratic.

The jungle takes over so quickly again.
The burnt-out beach huts are covered in plants,
and the wreck of a bus on the cliff road
is full of dark rustlings, and bones.
Each evening at sunset, a woman
brings three incense sticks to the shrine,
clasps her hands in prayer, and bows.

When all the spies have been recalled
and the 'historic incidents' reported
(perhaps a wave of executions in the capital,
but down here in the provinces, the journalists
were kept waiting for days without news),
when the trains have all wound their long ways north,
and the airports are pitted and overgrown again,
when even the newspapers have yellowed
and the telexes stopped chattering,
there will be no way out but patience
(I am talking of a long time from now).

READING MARCO POLO, AND REMEMBERING

I have been staring too long at the trees
in the mist, in this quiet country
where nothing ever happens:
but the price we pay now and then.

I must tell you that in this province...

and then at the end of the valley
a car's lights sweeping for miles

which is it? a hint of fear
or the glimmer of far peaks

trucks rattle past in the dark
like an ugly promise

mystery of shards of bone
dust storms wheel and swoop

ack-ack in the high blue
the mountains rumble echo

return of gunfire and it's all
a joke - playing you see

a few scared birds
and nomads swearing vengeance

and that's all?

Away back down the valley,
he says, with a shrug.

ON THE BORDERS OF WAR ?

Consider:

at this moment
in a wet seaside town
someone is walking
her bag filled with spices
saffron, coriander.
and the flash of red silk

contain this idea,   no
balance each perception
like that   yes

not much time left now
careful
how this moment relates
to our world

night seeping in past the clouds

MASSAGING THE FIGURES

"We need equipment, not enthusiasm"
was what they always replied.
The women returning from the front
were full of stories: amputations under fire,
tortured children screaming through the night,
and the dogs roaming the camps.

Beyond the hills, we could hear nothing.
The summer burned on: dust, and the days
drier and drier until all the water was rationed.
The trickle of refugees stopped.
There was no more news. Something
had happened. We stopped talking.

Later she remembered what they had heard:
the green of summer lay thick on the hills.
No sound but insects, no movement but butterflies.
As she rounded the corner, under the cool dark of trees
that formed a natural avenue, the air changed.
A different colour seemed to fill the sky.

She glimpsed the white city far off, on the plain,
through the heavy branches on the hillside
laden with fruit at the end of a long day's march.
Sometimes she heard a deep pulse from behind doors,
or when a window swung open, she heard laughter
billowing out into the street. An insistent heartbeat.

She could touch the strangeness of these shadows,
the faces passing through the dark, music
down an alley, the pull of the city: stone and iron
numbers in rows, the grids of pavement
reflecting the sky after rain, all these
vital links between the intellect and her emotions.

But these concepts were too big for her to handle:
she drove and drove, glancing at the signs
around her, a spinning cobweb of steel.
The winter light faded, snow dusted the sky.
White lines referenced her landscape,
the wire outlines of fences, trees.

Is it normal not to sleep when the rains come
with a crash and the roaring of winds,
the mountains rumble all night long
and we watch the electricity flicker
and the grey light dancing?
how the darkness keeps closing in and in.

Lie back, listen to the wind in the pines
beside the seas in your mind, the mountains
and the bleat of sheep moving slowly through the sun.
Which lines lead where? Out over the ocean,
beyond islands lit by sunshafts, the clouds are piling up,
rains scudding away from the light.

Now there will be silence beyond those mountains
and no travellers permitted to cross the borders.
A lazy rumble of rockfalls across the valley
as their whole history vanishes in weeks.
Here, staring at the flickering green screen,
storming the world of numbers, can we calculate all this?
(Smoke in the suburbs, sirens through the city dusk).

ATTEMPTING, OR

The important thing is to see and in not knowing what you understand
quite, take away the essentials till all that is left is
Phhh! and all that. So in essence what you have
between forefinger and thumb, leaving black streaks across
white sheets of lightning is it.

Now with the irreversible decline and the lack of common ground
it is becoming virtually impossible to maintain a dialogue
between those in power and those who feel disaffected
(he belched, quietly)

The glass of water upended on the table,
the postcard quickly removed,
a letter posted without a stamp
or marked 'Return to Sender'
what a pity

trunkcalls
cable TV
holograms

The only one of them with any sense was the weatherman.
At least he was honestly attempting to make sense
of random phenomena and hoping to convey
some kind of vision of the future
to a waiting, willing audience
but most switch off
(or keep the picture on with the sound down)

and beyond the hill as usual, the sea
playing its tricks of light,
the clouds recur and recur
and sometimes the sun
she said with great difficulty
gazing out of the window
at something I could not see
so I took her hand gently
and asked whether for this reason or
perhaps in the end
it matters that you
and if you should?

PERHAPS

Making the most of each moment
but
how hard sometimes
(even when it is dawn
over the old hills)
to see the place
you are
sitting in the window reading
dangling a piece of string
and the kitten tangling the end
over in the corner
while all around the windows
the storm rages

UNBELIEVABLE WEATHER

Ages of words
stretch to the horizon:

the technicalities of slick talk
fill your head with reasoned
argument
rhythms and metres of confidence

a single shot
kills the plot

Beyond the June hedgerow
(breeze off the sea
flowers dancing
passion of bees)

a plane hangs in the sky
ripping the blue apart

PEEPING TOM

Outside this room, the lies are spread
a little less thick.
Streets converge beneath my window.
Curtains parted, in the dark,
I watch the van arrive. They take him away.

Five minutes ago, I telephoned.
He was singing from the rooftops,
swaying from scaffolding,
I thought he would slip, plummet
to the pavement with a thump.
I did not want to hear his scream
arc down through the night; I am not interested
in experiments. I did not have the courage
to leave him up there, singing *Allelujah!*
If he'd fallen, he'd have jumped,
flown out over London like a dream,
New Year's Eve and the whole capital spread,
floating, beneath him.
I would have followed him
with my binoculars, mouth open.
I was not born to fly. I spy
out from behind curtains.
The van door swings to with a satisfying metallic
clunk.

ENDLESS ENTERTAINMENT

There is no comparison betwen the way you tell your stories and the way others, more established perhaps, give their versions of events. You must show trust, you see, and be able to follow your moods as they occur, go with them in whichever directions are required.

But when anger flares? The problem is spotting it far off, in the distance, like a plume of smoke on a hazy summer afternoon. Something of danger, or a hint of some untoward event, hanging like a reminder of the other times, there, beyond the wood, or on the hilltop. If it interrupts the holiday, or spoils the picnic, never mind, for there is some plan behind it all and your enquiry, your hesitation, is in order.

But now, suppose you wake one morning and see the white cupboards there as usual, and the nice pictures in their neat frames aligned just so along the walls, and the ripple of light through the curtains - but yet you cannot tell what woke you. What then? What to do? Was it the phone, or a car door slamming? Do you turn over to look at the time, or get up in alarm, groping for your clothes, at the thought of intruders.

Is it worth treading softly or otherwise taking care? Shouldn't you rather tiptoe to the phone, and dial hopefully, keeping your ear to the receiver as if you could will the operator to answer? But these old handcranked sets are strangely familiar, a far cry from the pushbutton digital ones at home. How can you suddenly unlearn the zip fly, and cope with buttons, buttons everywhere? Relearn the art of knotting a cravate? Or, handling servants - or even more difficult, waiting in attendance. No credit cards of course, and precious little cash. Could you cope with a Bill of Exchange? Has the language changed? It is no good reading the novels of the period, they only give you the refined essence of educated written prose. Suddenly you are stuck in a morass of vocabulary and accents you have never heard before, a cross between Mummerset and Cockney and something you had never expected, Afrikaans. A black man in the street, dressed in livery, and you suddenly realize, 'a slave!' The poor are begging in rags at the gate, but you are hardly allowed to look through the back window at them, let alone mention them in conversation. The whole thing is an elaborate façade, put there for your own 'protection'. Your host is a 'gentleman', considerate enough though rather aloof. You seem to be in the fashionable centre of a large town or city, though where exactly it is, you cannot tell. You catch one of the servants speaking in a Scottish accent, but dare not ask where she comes from, for fear of breaking the bounds of propriety. After dinner, you broach the subject. The company look at you as if you were mad, and you suddenly realize you have not looked in a mirror since your arrival. Perhaps that will give a clue as to your whereabouts.

What makes him tick? This man with the quiet obsessions, his books all ordered neatly in rows, dated, the domestic systems all neatly controlled and the photo albums ready for display at the touch of a finger, ready for posting. Where was I? Before the Wars, long before the invention of radio and TV, when night lasted all through the darkness, before even gaslamps had been installed, though some talked of the Fairey Lights of the Capital.

Il ne faut jamais tomber dans le désespoir. En effet.

Who said that? A fragment of French at the luncheon table. Strange how a detail at the corner of your eye, or a chance remark overhead amidst the hubbub can bring you back to Reality with a shock, though smells and scents usually send me away into a worried daydream as I try to recall exact moments of odour or taste. No, this will not do, we must settle down to business. Here we are then, once again seated round the dining room table with strangers, conducting bussiness in here because it is the largest room and easily accessible from the kitchens, with the constant demands on the servants to bring more freshly brewed coffee and tea. The sideboard glimmers.... oh, the delights of nostalgia. Steam! Varnished mahogany and brass fittings! The crisp turn of a perfectly starched cuff! The need to wash the knives in powder, the polishing cloths and beeswax, creak of real leather boots, the satisfying crackle of a real fire and good conversation.... and three postal deliveries a day across town, the quiet clip clop on cobbles.

Near the borders words move, shift sound, as wind in a tree, as the moon widens its arc and the light at 2 am is a very different scene from what I know of it at midday. They only let me look out once a day at a time I choose.

The anxieties of small things - where is that crow flying to? How long will that butterfly dance? Has anyone counted all the flowers? - add up to a huge pressing problem. The scale of it is all wrong. We treat large things as though they were small, and the small as if they were large. This is not good for our planet, nor for our morale.

And as for time! Lord, the strange obsessions of each generation. Time was when the summer day was longer than in winter, so the hours too varied in length. Like animals, we were sleeping more in the winter, and less in the summer, when there was more work to be done.

We live on the borders of words, where meanings shift, change their alignments and the powers that be move the various vocabularies around, to suit their meanings at that particular moment in time.

CALCULATIONS OF LOSS

Here in the courtyards of Europe
I live in an imaginary Africa.

Our lands: stone centuries weighing down the memories,
and as the millennia shift we feel a need to record:
bombed buildings, shattered brickwork, new holes in walls, roofs,
the latest war's scars on the town.

For all our fantastic philosophies, still
this urge to destroy, obliterate, return to zero.

Why this deadly price for Thought,
the inevitable Logic dragging us backwards?

Bullet-holed brick is politics made fact,
this ugly time where ideas are terror,
painted on beautiful landscapes, and the results
are Civiltà Virtù Onestà Filosofia

and corpses

stone-faced Europe waiting in the wings, forgetting
its lines, mumbling its entrances, the same mistakes:
the unlocked door, the window singing on rusty hinges
curtains rotting in the sun and fine dust sifted over the floor.
Years ago (but only weeks) they left.
The panic of departure, books, pots, pans
and pickle jars stacked in the dark against better days.
An ordinary cellar of jams and spices,
where mice have ripped the bags and sacks
of rice spilled on the stone

Calculations of loss, the endless sorrows of silence,
but improvisations of strength when iron clangs
and smoke drifts up through the valley stillness

all those forgotten sermons and the uncountable sums
the undeclined nouns and unravelled conjugations
corrections hidden away in boxes of books
and ragged piles of paper

(their vulnerability exposes our desires as shams,
what more do we want?

purple petals   white cows
floating down the avenue?   blocking the streets?

scent of flowers, tang of spices
the glimpses of ice on a distant skyline

where smiling crowds gather
can peace now be far off?)

THE WATCHMENDER

These long views are deceptive:
as she stares from the window
at the river, fields, and flow of clouds
across traditional landscapes, their meanings
are inconsistent

yesterday, the fields moved further away through the mist
tomorrow they will be right up close to the pane
in a dazzle of summer
and now, a bank of clouds glowing at sunset...

but full of hopes or fears, the landscape is changing with the wind,
the edges of lanes are adrift with flowers,
and the view comes alive in moonlight...

nightingales...

(a stroke of light
gesture of contact
across her face)

then grey banks of drizzle
sweep the valley
the light smears, smudges, clears
away downriver mud
shallows wait for flood

processions of herons
quarter the shallows
grey acres recede into mist,

ghost boats
tip their masts at the stars

(shadows of skin against firelight,
or amber in snow,
these gestures of faith
swaying smoke)

Old stone stands alone
against the elements

but how often do our gestures coincide?

(pretence of passion
stifles the soul)

rain on wind on walls against winter:
our answers

teeth of rocks
worn down
eaten by winters
wind rain frost

where speech fails
and tongues trip

or a leaf
finally
flutters to ground
parched
after weeks of waiting

(music
inexplicably
stopped)

instants of joy
scattered
among the twigs
like berries.

GROUND

so
   moving from piano
   with precision (on tiptoe)
       to an empty stave
(foolscap ready on the stand
in the corner of morning sunlight
   slanting between curtain and door)

I try not to wake the still
sleeping
household of potential listeners

on the hillside beyond the window
waving grass (it is early summer)
moves across the eye

a rustle of red petals on the terrace

I attempt music
or rather

the music repeating itself
on a circular tune
a simple melody

picked hesitantly
from a dream?

or remembered

at last

to see
        the footsteps across the terrace
        left after a night of snow
the trees below lining the river
a queue of dark strangers waiting
for the weather to change

'never rely on the spare matchbox'

thoughts stun:
if winter follows spring as surely
as autumn prepares these fields
for summer's crescendi of voices,
are there more certain ways
to predict crop circles?

WORLD CUP FINAL

The actors come and go, the singers strut, in multilayered disguises, even their voices change, the effect is magical.

The crowds rise, still clapping, the quicker ones grabbing their coats and making for the exit stairs already as the lead soprano takes another curtain call. Hopefully there won't be another encore, I wonder if there is still time to phone. Just.

Hopeless trying to get a taxi. I walk in the rain and cool down.

Not so bad after all.

The aria in act two could have been a bit faster, more colour perhaps on the high notes.

What about tomorrow? Always something to worry about. I press on homeward.

Settling for a final read of the day's paper, my eye catches the same small ad:

it's never the same number, but usually the same words. When I ring there's a 'number unobtainable' tone.

Off stage, they are preparing again.

Ought I to alert Central? My phone's tapped of course. This is too much. After all that has happened in Eastern Europe, you'd have hoped that kind of game was over, finally, the circle cut from the middle of the flag, the statues overturned, melted down.

But even in the middle of summer, here, at home, there is a chill wind blowing. If only we could tell where from.

Timers, lights go on and off at random.

So I settle down again and start to read, carefully this time, through the old notes. Diaries from years and years ago. A photo, an old stamp, a tube ticket, fall from the back of a notebook. I was heavier then than I remember.

This kind of thing can go on for ever.

Slacking off beyond the halfway line. Teapot on the sink drainer.

Light off the polished hubcap reflects his face in a round world: this kind of anxiety is normal. Illusions of depth, entertaining vast distances across the cosmos, the smaller planets left reeling. If only, if only, we could see just a little further.

Among leaflitter
searching with bags in hand
mushroom explosions

cliché angers me
elastic bands twang
smoke filled rooms

every venue new
each night might cheat
you of a few

moments of clarity:
the white pheasant
by the hedge

is real and no one
in his right mind
would shoot *that*.

Catchall detergent
wipes clean all surfaces
kills all *known* germs

Cholesterol? Clean as
a whistle you'll be
home by Christmas.

Religion on a plate. The meats steam. Liturgical softness of flicker and chant echoing round pillars and vaults. Eat, drink, be ACCURATE.

After a sleepless night
(heartbeat, heat,
the hoot of a long foreign train
across vast distances)

it would not be good morning without
first birdsong
then clean light
breaking through mist

along the top of the hill
each branch and leaf
sharp against the sky

the sun floating up on the haze
where yesterday I looked out to sea

white silence stretching to nothing

NO PLACE LIKE HOME

In flat lands
and mountain countries

I look out of windows
at the view but

that house on the hill
haunts me still:

the way it hides
behind trees

windows glinting
in the sun at odd

times of the day
like this

NO MORE THAN THAT

If you were to look
from the bedroom window
into their garden

nothing

just that you would be as
fascinated as
anyone else:
all gossip and lies.

HOW FAR IS IT NOW?

The promise
of that windblown rose
can be kept as long
as you like to look

that windblown rose in a cutglass vase

the secret
in the manner of its presentation

(but watch
the petals fold
fade, fall

and then the leaves droop
drop)

AND THAT'S ALL

To list your shortcomings
one after one
and then start again
counting the days left to you.

And after that violent night
to be woken by birdsong
and the smell of the sea
through the old window,
a view so familiar
it is almost like getting home.